# More
# Welsh Jokes

Dilwyn Phillips

yLolfa

First impression: 2005
Third impression: 2010

Copyright © Dilwyn Phillips & Y Lolfa 2005

*This book is subject to copyright and may not be reproduced by any
means except for review purposes without the prior, written consent
of the publishers.*

Cover and illustrations: Sion Jones

ISBN: 0 86243 784 9
ISBN-13: 9780862437848

Printed on acid-free and partly recycled paper
and published and bound in Wales by
Y Lolfa Cyf., Talybont, Ceredigion SY24 5HE
*e-mail* ylolfa@ylolfa.com
*website* www.ylolfa.com
*tel* (01970) 832 304
*fax* 832 782

# Contents

# Introduction

Following the publication of Welsh Jokes, people have continually asked for a second volume. This book follows the style set in the still-popular Welsh Jokes, with the addition of a few new characters and chapters, including a 'naughty' section – not for the under 21's.

Any similarity to anyone you know is purely coincidental... with the exception of Ianto, Dai, Myfanwy, Twm, Megan, and other Welsh people and sheep from your village or area.

The Welsh have maintained their sense of humour throughout the years despite being faced with hard times. Whilst on my usual travels around Wales, I encountered a railway porter once, and commented upon the rather long road to the station, to which he replied, "Sir, if it was any shorter, it wouldn't reach the train!"

The village idiot is naturally quick-witted. Only recently, whilst staying in a hotel near Llandrindod Wells, I noticed two statues of Alsatian dogs on top of the pillars at the entrance to the driveway leading to the Hotel. I winked at the porter and asked him how often he fed those dogs. Without hesitation he replied, "Only when they bark, sir!"

I hope you enjoy reading this book as much as you enjoyed the first, and if you haven't read the first, you can always read it second!

Dilwyn Phillips

# The Very Young

Two brothers, Emyr and Twm, were spending the night at their grandparents'. At bedtime, the two boys knelt beside their beds to say their prayers. Emyr began praying at the top of his lungs: "I PRAY FOR A NEW BICYCLE... I PRAY FOR A NEW GAMEBOY... I PRAY FOR A NEW DVD..."

Twm leaned over and nudged Emyr and said, "Why are you shouting your prayers? God isn't deaf!" To which Emyr replied, "No, but Gran is!"

\* \* \*

One day Bethan was sitting and watching her mother do the dishes at the kitchen sink. She suddenly noticed that her mother had several strands of white hair sticking out in contrast on her brunette head. She looked at her mother and inquisitively asked, "Why are some of your hairs white, Mum?"

Her mother replied, "Well, you see, Bethan, every time you do something wrong and make me cry or unhappy, one of my hairs turns white."

Bethan thought about this revelation for a while and then said, "Mum, how come ALL of Grandma's hairs are white?"

*   *   *

The maths teacher saw that Tomi bach wasn't paying attention in class. She called on him and said, "Tomi! What are 7, 3, 11 and 19?" Little Tomi quickly replied, "History channel, ITV, Discovery, and the Cartoon Network!"

*   *   *

Ianto was packing for his holidays and his 3-year-old son was having a wonderful time playing on the bed. At one point, little Emyr said, "Daddy, look at this," and stuck out two of his fingers.

Trying to keep him entertained, Ianto reached out and stuck his tiny fingers in his mouth and said, "Daddy's going to eat your fingers!" pretending to eat them before he rushed out of the room again.

When Ianto returned, little Emyr was standing on the bed

staring at his fingers with a devastated look on his face.

Ianto said, "What's wrong, cariad bach?"

Emyr replied, "What happened to my bogeys?"

\*    \*    \*

A three-year-old boy went with his father to see a new litter of kittens. On returning home, he breathlessly informed his mum, "There were two boy kittens and two girl kittens."

"How did you know that?" his mother asked.

"Daddy picked them up and looked underneath," he replied. "I think it's printed on the bottom."

\*    \*    \*

Little Tomos was in the garden, filling in a hole, when his neighbour peered over the fence.

Interested in what the cheeky-faced youngster was doing, he politely asked, "What are you up to there, Tomos?"

"Well, my goldfish died," replied Tomos tearfully, without looking up, "and I've just buried him."

The neighbour was concerned, "That's an awfully big hole for a goldfish, isn't it?"

Tomos patted down the last heap of earth then replied, "That's because he's inside your bloody cat!"

\*    \*    \*

Farmer Jones was helping one of his cows give birth, when he noticed Ithel, his 11-year-old son, standing wide-eyed at the fence, absolutely amazed with the whole event.

He thought, "Bloody Hell! Ithel's eleven now. I'm going to have to start telling him about the facts of life. At the moment though, I'll just let him ask, and I'll answer."

After everything was over, Farmer Jones walked over to him and said, "Well Ithel, any questions?"

"Just one, Dad," gasped Ithel. Just as his dad is preparing his birds and bees story, Ithel asks, "How fast was that calf going when he hit that cow?"

\* \* \*

Little Ruth came home from school and smelled alcohol on her mother's breath.

"Daddy's going to be annoyed with you, Mam," she said, "you've been using his perfume again!"

\* \* \*

While working for meals-on-wheels, delivering lunches to the elderly, Megan used to take her four-year-old daughter Morfydd on her afternoon rounds. She was unfailingly intrigued by the various appliances of old age, particularly the canes, walkers and wheelchairs. One day little Morfydd was staring at a pair of false teeth soaking in a glass. As Megan braced herself for the inevitable barrage of questions, Morfydd merely turned and whispered, "The tooth fairy will never believe this!"

\* \* \*

Young Marged was walking home from school, and the weather that afternoon was pretty rough. Thunder clouds were forming. As the afternoon progressed, the winds whipped up – along with thunder came lightning. Her mother felt rather concerned that Marged would be frightened, and she also thought that the electrical storm might hurt little Marged. Following the roar of thunder, lightning would cut through the sky like a flaming sword. Full of concern, her mum quickly got in her car and drove to meet her. As she did, she saw little Marged walking along, but at each flash of lightning, Marged would stop, look up and smile. Further flashes of lightning followed in quick succession, and each time, Marged would stop, look up and smile. When Marged's mum stopped the car, she asked, "What are you doing, Megan?" Megan answered, "Smiling! God just keeps taking pictures of me!"

\* \* \*

One morning at church, Mr Jones was preaching about what God was and wasn't.

He said "God is neither white nor black. God is neither male nor female."

After hearing all this, Tomos, a curious 5-year-old turned to his dad and asked, "Daddy, is God Michael Jackson?"

\* \* \*

Finding one of her nursery kids making faces at others on the playground, Miss Jones stopped to gently reprove the child. Smiling sweetly, the teacher said, "Tomi, when I was a child, I was told that if I made an ugly face, it would freeze and I would stay like that." Tomi looked up and replied, "Well, Miss Jones, you can't say you weren't warned!"

* * *

Miss James was working with a group of children in a valleys school, trying to broaden their horizons through taste. She brought in a variety of foods and said, "Right, children. I'd like you to close your eyes and taste these."

The kids easily recognised the taste of cherries, lemons and mint, but when the teacher gave them some honey, they were all stumped.

"I'll give you a little clue," said the teacher. "It's something your mum calls your dad sometime."

Instantly, little Sue spat the sticky substance out and shouted, "Ych a fi, spit 'em out – they're assholes!"

* * *

Little Tomos's mother asked him to make tea, when Mrs Jones next door called in one day. When she looked in to check on him in the kitchen, his mother noticed that Tomos had already strained the tea. So the two neighbours sipped their tea happily and chit-chatted.

Afterwards, when Mrs Jones next door had left, Tomos's mother asked him, "Did you have any problems finding the tea strainer?"

"Mam, I couldn't find it, so I used the fly swatter," replied Tomos. His mother nearly fainted, so Tomos quickly added, "Don't get excited, Mam, I used the old one!"

* * *

Tomos loved to help his mam. One evening, he set the table when company was due for dinner. Soon Mr Jones, the guest, arrived and everyone sat down to eat.

Then Mother noticed something was missing…

"Tomos, cariad," she said, "You didn't put a knife and fork at Mr Jones's place."

"But, Mammy, I thought he wouldn't need them," explained Tomos. "Daddy says he always eats like a horse!"

\*   \*   \*

Tomi bach said, "When I die, I want to die like my grandfather, who died peacefully in his sleep, not screaming like all the passengers that were riding with him in his car!"

\*   \*   \*

Tomos was talking to his teacher about whales. The teacher said it was physically impossible for a whale to swallow a human because even though it was a very large mammal its throat was very small.

Tomos stated that Jonah was swallowed by a whale. Irritated, the teacher reiterated that a whale could not swallow a human; it was physically impossible.

"When I get to heaven I will ask Jonah," Tomos said.

"What if Jonah went to hell?" the teacher asked,

Tomos replied, "Well, then – you ask him!"

\*   \*   \*

A Nursery teacher was observing her classroom of children while they were drawing. She occasionally walked around to see each child's work.

As she got to Tomos, who was working diligently, she asked what the drawing was.

Tomos replied, "I'm drawing God."

The teacher paused and said, "But Tomos, no one knows what God looks like."

Without missing a beat, or looking up from his drawing, Tomos replied, "They will in a minute."

\* \* \*

Little Tomi was auditioning for a school play. He won a part and went home to tell his father.

His father was really proud of him. So his father asks, "What part did you get?

Tomi replied, "I got the part of a man who has been married for 25 years."

His father congratulated him. And then he said, "That's good, Tomi. Maybe next time you'll get a talking role!"

\* \* \*

A Sunday school teacher was discussing the Ten Command ments with her class of six-year-olds. After explaining the commandment to 'honour thy father and thy mother', she asked, "Is there a commandment that teaches us how to treat our brothers and sisters?"

Without missing a beat Tomos (the eldest of a family) answered, "Thou shall not kill."

# School

Geraint, having just received his GCSE results, came home from school rather depressed.

"What's the matter, Geraint bach?" asked his mum.

"Mammy," said Geraint, "It's my marks. They're all wet."

"What do you mean, all wet?"

"Below C-level!"

\* \* \*

The children were lined up in the cafeteria of a Catholic elementary school for lunch. At the head of the table was a large pile of apples. The nun made a note, and posted it on the apple tray: "Take only ONE. God is watching."

Moving further along the lunch line, at the other end of the table was a large pile of chocolate chip cookies. Tomi had written a note: "Take all you want. God is watching the apples."

\* \* \*

According to an education report, a certain comprehensive school in Wales was recently faced with a problem. A number of year-12 girls were beginning to use lipstick and would put it on in the toilets. That was alright, but after they put on their lipstick they would press their lips to the mirror, leaving dozens of little lip prints.

Every night, the cleaners would remove them, and the next day, the girls would put them back.

Finally the Headmaster decided that something had to be done. He called all the girls to the toilets and met them there with the caretaker.

He explained that all these lip prints were causing a big problem for the school cleaners, who had to clean the mirrors every night. To show how difficult it had been to clean the mirrors, he asked the caretaker to show the girls how much effort was required.

The caretaker took a long-handled squeegee, dipped it in the toilet, and cleaned the mirror with it.

Since then, there have been no lip prints on the mirror.

\*　　\*　　\*

Miss Jones, the Biology teacher, asked her class what they knew about the birds and the bees. With that, Barry started crying.

"What's wrong, Barry?" asked Miss Jones.

"Miss," he replied, "when I was eight, I was told that there was no Father Christmas. When I was nine, I was told that there was no Easter bunny. When I was ten, I was told that there was no tooth fairy, and I suppose now you're going to tell me that grown ups don't really have sex. There's nothing left to live for now!"

\*　　\*　　\*

**Gone are the days of whispering of answers...**

One day, Miss Jones told her class that they were not to use childish words, and insisted that no baby talk was allowed, only grown-up words. She asked Emyr bach what he had done over the weekend.

"Please Miss," he answered, "I went to visit my nana."

"No," said Miss Jones, "you went to visit your grand-mother. You must learn to use grown-up words." She then asked Bethan what she had done.

"Please Miss," answered Bethan, "I went for a ride on the choo-choo."

"No, Bethan," corrected Miss Jones, you went for a ride on the train. You must learn to use grown-up words. Is that clear?"

"What did you do, Gareth?" she asked.

"Please Miss, I read a book," replied Gareth.

"Good," said Miss Jones. "What did you read, Gareth bach?"

Gareth thought for a moment, and said, "Winnie the Shit!"

*　*　*

It was teacher's birthday, so every child in the class was giving her a special birthday present.

Ann's mother owned a flower shop, so Ann gave the teacher some beautiful flowers.

Emyr's parents owned a sweet shop, so Emyr gave the teacher a wonderful box of chocolates.

Then it was little Tomos's turn. Tomos's father owned a wine shop, and Tomos brought a big box for his teacher. When he handed the box to his teacher, she noticed that the bottom of the box was wet. So she put her finger on it and tasted.

"Is it wine?" the teacher asked.

"No, it's not wine!" Tomos replied.

She tasted it again. "Hmmmmmm. Is it some sort of spirit?"

"Nope, it's not a spirit!" said Tomos.

She tasted it again and was puzzled. "Well, Tomos, I give up. What is it?"

Tomos was excited, and said with a big smile. "It's a puppy, miss!"

*　*　*

The teacher asked little Tomos if he knows his numbers.

"Yes," he said, "I do. My dad taught me."

"Good. What comes after three?"

"Four," answered Tomos.

"What comes after six?"

"Seven."

"Very good," says the teacher. "Your dad did a good job. What comes after ten?"

"A Jack."

\*　　\*　　\*

In his essay, Morgan stated: "The girl tumbled down the stairs and lay prostitute at the bottom."

In the margin of the paper, the English teacher commented: "My dear Morgan Evans, you must learn to distinguish between a fallen woman and one who has merely slipped."

\*　　\*　　\*

A teacher was giving a lesson on the circulation of the blood.

Trying to make the matter clearer, she said, "Now, class, if I stood on my head, the blood, as you know, would run into it, and I would turn red in the face."

"Yes," the class said.

"Then why is it that while I am standing upright in the ordinary position, the blood doesn't run into my feet?"

Tomos shouted, "'Cause your feet ain't empty!"

\*　　\*　　\*

# Bars

Dai was sitting at a bar, just looking at his drink. He waited like that for half an hour. Then this big trouble-making miner, Wil, goes up to him, takes the drink from Dai's glass, and drinks it all down. Dai starts to cry.

"Come on Dai, I was just joking," said Wil. "Here, I'll buy you another drink. I just can't stand to see a man crying."

"No, it's not that. This is the worst day of my life. First, I fall asleep, and I'm late to my office. My boss, really bloody annoyed, sacks me. As soon as I leave the building, to go to my car, I find out that someone's stolen it. The police say they can't do anything. I caught a taxi home, and when I got out, I remember I left my wallet and credit cards in it, but the taxi had already gone. I eventually got home, and as soon as I get inside, I find my wife in bed with the gardener. I leave home and come to this bar. And as soon as I think about putting an end to my life, you show up and drink my poison …"

*    *    *

Ifan goes into the bar and sits down and orders a drink. Other than the barman, there's no-one else in the place. All of a sudden a voice says, "Nice suit." Ifan looks around and doesn't see anyone, and the barman looks busy washing some glasses. Sometime later, the same voice says, "Nice tie." Ifan looks around again and doesn't see anyone. He now asks the barman if he just said something.

"No," replied the barman, "it wasn't me. It was probably the peanuts – they're complimentary."

*    *    *

A very attractive Marged goes up to the bar in a quiet pub. She gestures alluringly to the barman who comes over immediately.

When he arrives, she seductively signals that he should bring his face closer to hers. When he does, she begins to gently caress his full beard.

"Are you the boss?' Marged asks, softly stroking his face with both hands.

"Well, no," he replied.

"Can you get him for me? I need to speak to him," she says, running her hands beyond his beard and into his hair.

"Well," drools the barman, "it's quite inconvenient, but I'm sure I can help you instead."

"I need you to give him a message," she continues, running her forefingers across the barman's lips and shyly popping a couple of fingers into his mouth and allowing him to suck them gently.

"What should I tell him?" the barman manages to say.

"Tell him," Marged whispers, "there's no toilet paper, soap, or towels in the ladies' toilet !"

\* \* \*

Walking into the White Lion, Andy said to the barman, "Pour me a stiff one – I just had another fight with the old lady."

"Oh yeah?" said the barman. "And how did this one end?"

"When it was all over," Andy replied, "she came to me on her hands and knees."

"Really? Now that's a switch! What did she say?" asked John.

She said, "Come out from under that bed, you little chicken shit!"

\* \* \*

An Englishan, an Irishman, and a Welshman were in a pub, talking about their sons.

"My son was born on St George's Day," commented the Englishman. "So we obviously decided to call him George."

"That's a coincidence," remarked the Welshman. "My son was born on St David's Day, so obviously we decided to call him David."

"That's incredible! What a coincidence!" said the Irishman. "Exactly the same thing happened with my son, Pancake!"

\*   \*   \*

Dai and Ianto were in the White Horse enjoying a pint when they decided to get in on the weekly draw. They bought five tickets each for a pound. The following week when the raffle was drawn, both had won a prize.

Dai won first prize: a year's supply of gourmet spaghetti sauce and extra-long spaghetti.

Ianto won sixth prize: a toilet brush.

About a week or so had passed when the men met back in the White for a couple of pints.

Ianto asked Dai how he liked his prize, to which Dai replied, "Great, I love spaghetti!"

"Ianto !" asked Dai, " how about you, how's the toilet brush?"

"Not so good," replied Ianto. " I think I'll go back to using paper."

\*   \*   \*

"My god! What happened to you?" John the barman asked Andy as he hobbled into the White Lion on a crutch, one arm in plaster.

"I got in a fight with Dai Jones."

"Dai Jones? He's only a small chap," John said, surprised. "He must have had something in his hand."

"He did," Andy said. "A shovel, it was."

"Dear Lord, Andy! Didn't you have anything in your hand?"

"Aye, that I did – Mrs Jones's left tit," Andy replied. "And a beautiful thing it was, but not much use in a fight!"

\*   \*   \*

A lun walks into the bar of the White with a tortoise in his hand. The tortoise's one eye is black and blue, two of his legs are bandaged, and his whole shell is taped together with insulating tape.

John the barman looks at Alun and asks: "What's wrong with your tortoise?"

"Notning," Alun replies. "This tortoise of mine is faster than your dog!"

"Not a chance!," replies the John.

"Okay then, says Alun… you take your dog and let him stand at one end of the bar near the telly. Then go and stand by the dartboard and call your dog. I'll bet you £25 that before your dog reaches you, my tortoise will be there."

John, thinking it's an easy £25, agrees. He goes to the other side of the bar near the telly, and on the count of three calls his dog.

Suddenly Alun picks up his tortoise and throws it across the room, narrowly missing John, and smashing it into the wall.

"I WIN… told you it'll be there before your dog!"

\*   \*   \*

Cyril, completely inebriated, walked into a bar and, after staring for some time at the only woman seated at the bar, walked over to her, placed his hand up her skirt and began fondling her.

She jumped up and slapped him silly.

Cyril immediately apologized and explained, "I'm sorry. I thought you were my wife. You look exactly like her."

"Why you drunken, worthless, insufferable asshole!" she screamed.

"That's funny," Cyril replied, "you sound exactly like her, too!"

# The Welsh Salesman

Wil had a reputation as a fantastic salesman. One day he visited a large department store in Cardiff and said to the manager, "This computer will cut your workload by 50%."

To which the Manager replied, "That's great, I'll take two of them!"

*   *   *

Andy goes along to the Patent Office in Newport with some of his new designs. He says to the assistant, "I'd like to register my new invention. It's a folding bottle."

"OK," says the assistant. "What do you call it?"

"A fottle, replies Andy."

"A fottle? That's a stupid! Can't you think of something else?"

"I can think about it. I've got something else, though," says Andy. "A folding carton."

"And what do you call that?" asks the assistant.

"A farton," replies Andy.

"That's rude. You can't possibly call it that!"

"In that case," says Andy, "you're really going to hate the name of my folding bucket!"

*   *   *

A woman saw an ad in the South Wales Gazette which read: "Purebred Police Dog, £50. Apply Bridgend Police HQ."

Thinking that to be a great bargain, she called in at Bridgend HQ and ordered the dog to be delivered to her valleys home. The next day a Black Maria arrived at her home and delivered the mangiest-looking mongrel she had ever seen. In a rage, she telephoned Bridgend HQ, and said, "How dare you call that mangy-mutt a purebred police dog?"

"Don't let his looks deceive you, madam," the dog handler replied, "He's in the Secret Service."

*   *   *

A police dog responds to an ad for work with the South Wales Force.

"Well," says the Chief, "you'll have to meet some strict requirements. First, you must type at least 60 words per minute." Sitting down at the typewriter, the dog types out 80 words per minute.

"Also," says the Chief, "you must pass a physical and complete the obstacle course." This perfect canine specimen finished the course in record time.

"There's one last requirement," the Chief concluded, "you must be bilingual." With confidence, the dog looks up at him and says, "Meow!"

\*　　\*　　\*

There are 3 people walking down the street: the perfect Welsh man, the perfect Welsh woman, and Mickey Mouse. They see a £50 note on the street. Who picks it up?

The perfect woman (naturally), because the other two are fictional characters!

\*　　\*　　\*

Dai knocks on a door, and unknown to him, a nun is undressing for a bath inside and she's standing naked. The nun calls, "Who is it?"

Dai answers, "A blind salesman".

The nun decides to get a thrill by having the blind man in the room while she's naked so she lets Dai in. Dai walks in, looks straight at the nun and says, "Er, can I sell you a blind, cariad?"

*   *   *

It was Christmas and the judge was in a merry mood as he asked Ianto, the defendant, "What are you charged with?"

"Doing my Christmas shopping early, sir," replied Ianto.

"Well, that's not a crime!" said the judge. "How early were you shopping?"

"Before the store opened," answered Ianto.

*   *   *

Evan starts a job as a door-to-door vacuum-cleaner salesman and manages to bull his way into a woman's home in the valleys.

"This machine is the best ever," he exclaims, whilst pouring a bag of dirt over the lounge floor.

The woman says she's really worried it may not all come off, so Evan says, "If this machine doesn't remove all the dust completely, I'll lick it off myself."

"Do you want ketchup on it?" she says. "We're not connected for electricity yet!"

*   *   *

Dai and Ianto, two bored casino dealers, were waiting at a table in a Cardiff casino.

A very attractive lady arrived and bet a thousand pounds on a single roll of the dice. She said, " I hope you don't mind, but I feel much luckier when I'm nude."

With that, she stripped from her neck down, rolled the dice and yelled, "By damn, I need new clothes!"

Then she shouted, "YES! YES! I WON! I WON!"

She jumped up and down and hugged both dealers. With that she picked up all the money and clothes and quickly departed. Dai stared at Ianto, dumbfounded.

Finally, Dai asked Ianto, "What did she roll?"

Ianto replied,"I thought YOU were watching!"

\* \* \*

Dai takes his car back to the garage and complains to the salesman that the car he'd bought there had a transvestite engine.

"Surely," said the salesman, "you mean a transverse engine."

"No," said Dai, "a transvestite engine – it has a habit of slipping into the wrong gear…"

\* \* \*

Little Myfanwy walks into a pet shop and asks in the sweetest little lisp:

"Excuthe me, mithter, do you keep wittle wabitths?" And the shopkeeper gets down on his knees, so that he's on her level, and asks: "Do you want a wittle white wabby or a soft and fuwwy bwack wabby?" She in turn puts her hands on her knees, bends forward and says, "I don't fink my pyfon gives a damn!"

\* \* \*

When young Gareth, a Rhondda salesman, met an untimely end, he was informed that he had a choice regarding where he would spend his eternity: Heaven or Hell. He was allowed to visit both places, and then make his decision afterwards.

"I'll see Heaven first," said Gareth, and an angel led through the gates on a private tour. Inside it was very peaceful and serene, and everybody was playing harps and eating grapes. It looked very nice, but Gareth was not about to make a decision that could very well condemn him to a life of musical produce.

"Can I see Hell now?" he asked. The angel pointed him to the lift, and he went down to the basement, where he was greeted by one of Satan's loyal followers. For the next half hour, Gareth was led through a tour of what appeared to be the best night clubs he'd ever seen. People were partying loudly, and having – if you'll pardon the expression – a hell of a time.

When the tour ended, Gareth was sent back up, where the angel asked him if he had reached a final decision.

"Yes, I have," he replied. "As great as Heaven looks and all, I have to admit that Hell was more of my kind of place. I've decided to spend my eternity down there."

Gareth was sent to hell, where he was immediately thrown into a cave, chained to a wall, and subjected to various tortures.

"When I came down here for the tour," he yelled with anger and pain, "I was shown a whole bunch of bars and parties and other great stuff! What happened?!"

The devil replied, "Oh, that! That was just the Sales Demo."

*   *   *

How can you tell when a salesperson is lying? His lips are moving.

*   *   *

Three harp makers from Llanelli have all been in business for years on the same block in the town. After years of a peaceful co-existence, the Jones family decided to put a sign in the window saying: "We make the best harps in Llanelli."

The Davies family soon followed suit, and put a sign in their window proclaiming: "We make the best harps in the world."

Finally, the Thomas family put a sign out at their shop saying: "We make the best harps on the block."

*   *   *

Twm, a super salesman from Cardigan who was out of his home territory had a heart attack in his hotel room in Cardiff and died. The hotel manager called Twm's boss in Cardigan and informed him of Twm's tragedy.

The company sales manager received the news in a nonchalant manner and instructed the hotel manager, "Return his samples by Parcel Force and search his pockets for orders."

*   *   *

At a prestigious auction in Cardigan, the bidding was intense and cut-throat. The room was filled with scowling Cardis, each determined to exploit any advantage at the expense of another. Without warning, Mr Evans the auctioneer paused the sale and announced, "A gentleman in this room has lost a wallet containing £10,000. If it is returned, he will pay a reward of £500."

There was a moment's silence, and then from the crowd came the cry,

"Five hundred and fifty!"

# Work

Dai walks into the local employment office, marches straight up to the counter and says, "Hi. You know, I just HATE drawing dole money. I'd rather have a job."

The assistant behind the counter says, "Your timing is excellent. We just got a job opening from a very wealthy old man who wants a chauffeur/bodyguard for his beautiful daughter. You'll have to drive around in his Mercedes, and of course, he'll supply all of your clothes. And because of the long hours, meals will be provided. You'll also be expected to escort her on luxurious overseas trips. You'll have a two-bedroom apartment above the garage. The starting salary is £20,000 a year."

Dai replied, "You're bloody kidding me!"

The assistant says, "Yeah, well, Dai, you started it."

*   *   *

A man is at his lawyer's funeral and and is surprised by the turnout for this one man. He turns to the people around him. "Why are you all at this man's funeral?"

A man turns towards him and says, "We're all clients."

"And you ALL came to pay your respects? How touching."

"No, we came to make sure he was dead."

*   *   *

A car was involved in an accident in Penarth. As expected, a large crowd gathered.

A newspaper reporter, anxious to get his story, could not get near the car. Being a clever sort, he started shouting loudly, "Let me through! Let me through! I'm the son of the victim!"

The crowd made way for him. Lying in front of the car was a donkey.

\* \* \*

Dai was driving down the M4 at a rather fast pace, but feeling secure in a line of cars all going at the same speed.

However, as they passed a radar trap, he got nailed and was pulled over.

The police officer handed him the report, received his signature and was about to walk away when the Dai asked him,

"Officer, I know I was speeding, but I don't think it's fair – there were plenty of other cars around me going just as fast, so why did you give me the ticket?"

"Did you ever go fishing?" the policeman asked Dai.

"Er… yes," Dai replied.

"Did you ever catch all the fish?"

\* \* \*

Ianto, a lorry driver, was driving along. A sign comes up that reads "low bridge ahead." Before Ianto knows it, the bridge is right ahead of him and he gets stuck under it. Cars are backed up for miles.

Finally, the police arrive. The policeman gets out of his car and walks around to Ianto, puts his hands on his hips and says, "Got stuck?"

Ianto replies, "No, mate. I was delivering this bridge and ran out of petrol."

\* \* \*

There was this man who was in a horrible accident, and was injured. But the only permanent damage he suffered was the amputation of both of his ears. As a result of this unusual handicap, he became very self-conscious of his affliction.

Because of the accident, he received a large sum of money from the insurance company. It was always his dream to own his own business; with all this money, he now had the means to do so. So he went out and purchased a small, but expanding, computer firm. But he realized that he had no business knowledge at all, so he decided to hire someone to run the business.

He interviewed three top candidates.

The first interview went really well. He really liked Dai. His last question for this first candidate was, "Do you notice anything unusual about me?" Dai said, "Now that you mention it, you have no ears."

The man got really upset and threw Dai out.

The second interview went even better than the first. This candidate, Evan, was much better than the first. Again, to conclude the interview, the man asked the same question again, "Do you notice anything unusual about me?"

"Yes, you have no ears."

The man was really upset again, and threw this second candidate out.

Then came the third interview. Ianto was even better than the second candidate, the best out of all of them. Almost certain that he wanted to hire Ianto, the man once again asked, "Do you notice anything unusual about me?"

Ianto replied, "Yes, I bet you are wearing contact lenses."

Surprised, the man then asked, "Wow! That's quite perceptive of you! How could you tell?"

Ianto burst out laughing and said, "You can't wear glasses if you don't have any ears!"

*   *   *

An accountant from Aberaeron dies and goes to heaven. He reaches the pearly gates and is amazed to see a happy crowd all waving banners and chanting his name. After a few minutes, St. Peter comes running across and says, "I'm sorry I wasn't here to greet you personally. God is looking forward to meeting such a remarkable man as yourself."

The accountant is perplexed.

"I've tried to lead a good life, but I am overwhelmed by your welcome," he tells St. Peter.

"It's the least we can do for someone as special as yourself. Imagine living to the age of 160 and still looking so young," says St. Peter. The man looks even more dumbfounded and replies, "160? I don't know what you mean. I'm only 40."

St. Peter replies, "But that can't be right – we've seen your time sheets!"

*   *   *

Three butties were working on a high rise building project: Wil, Twm and Ianto. Wil falls off and is killed instantly. As the ambulance takes the body away, Twm says, "Someone should go and tell his wife."

Ianto says, "OK, I'm pretty good at that sensitive stuff, I'll do it." Two hours later, he comes back carrying a six-pack.

Twm says, "Where did you get that, Ianto?"

"Wil's wife gave it to me."

"That's unbelievable! You told the lady her husband was dead and she gave you the beer?"

Ianto says, "Well not exactly. When she answered the door, I said to her, 'You must be Wil's widow'."

She said, "'No, I'm not a widow."

And I said, "Wanna bet me a six-pack?"


Three paramedics were sipping tea in a hospital canteen and were all boasting about improvements in their respective ambulance team's response times. "Since we installed our new satellite navigation system," bragged one, "we've cut our emergency response time by ten percent."

"Not bad," the second paramedic commented. "But by using a computer model of traffic patterns, we cut our average time by twenty percent."

"That's nothing," said Ianto, the third paramedic. "Since our ambulance driver passed his driving test, we've cut our emergency response time in half!"

\*   \*   \*

It was so cold last winter that I saw a lawyer with his hands in his own pockets.

* * *

Ianto wrote a note and placed it under his windscreen wiper and dashed off:

"I've driven around the block for 20 minutes. I'm late for an appointment, and if I don't park here I'll lose my job... Forgive us our trespasses."

On returning, he came back, only to find a parking ticket and this note:

"I've walked around the block for 20 years, and if I don't give you a ticket, I'll lose my job... Lead us not into temptation."

* * *

It was snowing heavily and blowing to the point that visibility was almost zero when Wendy went to work.

She made her way to the car and wondered how she was going to make it home.

She sat in her car while it warmed up and thought about her situation. She finally remembered her dad's advice that if she got caught in a blizzard, she should wait for a snowplough to come by and follow it. That way she would not get stuck in a snow drift. This made her feel much better, and sure enough, in a little while a snowplough went by, and she started to follow it.

As she followed the snowplough, she was feeling very smug as they continued, and she was not having any problem with the blizzard conditions.

After quite some time had passed, she was somewhat surprised when the snowplough stopped and the driver got out and came back to her car and signalled her to open her window.

The snowplough driver wanted to know if she was all right, as she had been following him for a long time.

She said that she was fine and told him of her dad's advice to follow a snowplough if she ever got caught in a snowstorm.

The driver replied that it was OK with him, and she could continue if she wanted… but he was done with the Asda's car park and was going over to Sainsbury's next.

# Country Folk

A gentleman from London was visiting a small farm near Dinas Mawddwy, and during this visit he saw a farmer feeding pigs in a most extraordinary way. The farmer would lift a pig up to a nearby apple tree, and the pig would eat the apples off the tree directly. The farmer would move the pig from one apple to another until the pig was satisfied, then he would start again with another pig. The city gent watched the activity for quite a while and was absolutely astonished. Finally, he could not resist saying to the farmer, "This is the most inefficient method of feeding pigs that I can imagine. Just think of the time that would be saved if you simply shook the apples off the tree and let the pigs eat them from the ground!" The farmer looked puzzled and replied, "What's time to a pig?"

\* \* \*

A young lady from Llanbrynmair was worried about her habit of biting her fingernails down to the quick, and was advised by a friend to take up yoga. She did so, and soon her fingernails were growing normally. Her friend asked her if yoga had totally cured her nervousness. "No," she replied, "but now I can reach my toe-nails, so I bite them instead."

\* \* \*

Dai was an insomniac agnostic dyslexic. He stayed up all night wondering if there really was a dog.

*   *   *

Geraint turned to Aled and said "Losing a wife can be hard. In my case it was almost bloody impossible!"

*   *   *

Enid passed away and Griff called 999. The emergency operator told Griff that she would send someone out right away.

"Where do you live?" asked the operator.

Griff replied, "At the end of Chalybeate Street, Llanbrynmair."

The operator asked, "Can you spell that for me?"

There was a long pause and finally Griff said, "How 'bout if I drag her over to Oak Street and you pick her up there?"

*   *   *

A farmer from Llanbrynmair grew peas. He was doing pretty well, but he was disturbed by some local kids who would sneak into his garden at night and eat his young peas.

After some careful thought, he came up with a clever idea that he thought would scare the kids away for sure. So he made up a sign and posted it in the field. The next day the kids showed up and they saw his sign: "Warning, one of the pea plants has been peed on."

The next day the farmer turned up to look over the field and he noticed to his delight that no peas were missing. He was perplexed, however, by a sign next to his. He drove his tractor up to the sign which read: "Now there are two!"

\*     \*     \*

There was once a farmer called Gerwyn who lived just outside Dolgellau and was extremely sad with life because people always made fun of him. He decided to do something about it.

Suddenly he thought – "I have never seen anyone making fun of Cardiff boys. So, if I start talking and behaving like them, no one will be able to make out that I am a man from the hills and make fun of me."

He went into isolation for three months and after a lot of practice, he walked confidently into a shop and said, "I'm bloody starving. Give me a Clark's pie and no jam on the pie, like."

Immediately, the man behind the counter said, "Are you from the hills?" Gerwyn was taken aback and he repeated his request. The man behind the counter said, "Are you from the hills or not?"

Gerwyn was finally very ashamed and amazed at the shop owner's discerning ability and so he admitted to the fact, after which he asked, "But how did you know?"

The shopkeeper replied, "This is a Chemist!"

\*     \*     \*

Soon after Jack clocked in for work, the foreman called him over and told him that he had a phone call in the front office. When Jack returned, he had a mournful expression on his face and his head hung low. His foreman noticed and asked if he had received bad news.

"Yes, it was, Boss" he replied, "I just found out that my mother died earlier this morning."

"Bloody Hell, that's awful," replied the foreman. "Do you want the rest of the day off?"

"No," replied Jack. "I'll finish the day out."

About an hour later, the foreman returned to inform him that there was another phone call for him up front. This time when Jack returned he looked twice as glum and the foreman asked if everything was alright.

"Boss, this has to be the worst day of my life," moaned Jack. "That was my brother, and his mother died today too!"

\* \* \*

Two old ladies were waiting for a bus to Machynlleth, and one of them was smoking a cigarette. It started to rain, so the old lady reached into her purse, took out a condom, cut off the tip and slipped it over her cigarette and continued to smoke.

Her friend saw this and said, "Hey that's a good idea! What is it that you put over your cigarette?" The other old lady said, "It's a condom. I use them to keep my cigarettes dry in the rain."

"A condom? Where do you get those?"

The lady with the cigarette told her friend that you could purchase condoms at the Chemist's.

When the two old ladies arrived in Mach, the old lady with all the questions went straight into the Chemist's shop and asked the assistant if he sold condoms.

The assistant said yes, but looked a little surprised that this old woman was interested in condoms, so he asked her, "What size do you want?"

"One that would fit a Camel."

*   *   *

Dyfrig, a lonely, elderly widower loved his cat so dearly that he tried to teach it to talk.

"If I can get Pws to talk with me," he reasoned, "I won't have to bother with ordinary people at all!" First, he tried feeding the cat a diet of canned salmon, then one of canaries. Pws obviously loved both, but still wouldn't learn to talk. Then, one day, several years after he had begun the project, Dyfrig had two parrots cooked in olive oil and served to Pws with asparagus and sauted potatoes. Pws eagerly licked the plate clean. Then, wonder of wonders, Pws suddenly turned to Dyfrig and shouted, "Look out!" The startled Dyfrig just stared at Pws in shock. He didn't move a muscle. Suddenly, the ceiling caved in and buried the poor fellow, but Pws survived by jumping out of the way. The cat shook her head in disgust and said, "Eight years he spends trying to get me to talk and then, when I do, the idiot doesn't listen."

*   *   *

One day Dyfrig decided to visit his friend Ithel and ask him for a favour.

"Ithel, my old bytti," he said. "I'm going on holiday for a few weeks and I wanted to know if you could come around a couple a times a day to check up on my elderly mam, and feed my cat."

"Dim problem," replied Ithel. "You go and have a good time."

So the next day Dyfrig left and headed for sunny Spain. However, after a week, he received a phone call from Ithel.

"Everything's ok over here," he said. "Except your cat. It's dead!"

"Bloody Hell," replied Dyfrig. "You could have been a bit more sensitive, Ithel!"

"What do you mean?" replied Ithel.

"Well, one day you could have rang me up and told me that my cat has climbed the tree. The next day you could tell me that it has gone even higher up the tree and refuses to come down. On the third day you could tell me that the cat lost its grip and fell from the tree and had to be taken to the vet because of a broken leg. Then on the fourth day you could have told me that it died peacefully in the vet clinic," explained Dyfrig.

So Ithel apologised and another week went by, then Dyfrig got another phone call from Ithel.

"All right, Dyfrig," he said. "Everything's ok here, except your mam – she's climbed the tree and refuses to come down!"

\* \* \*

Mike's grandfather clock suddenly stops working right one day, so he loads it into his van and takes it to a clock repair shop.

In the shop is a little old Swiss man with a heavy German accent. He asks Mike, "Vat seems to be ze problem?"

Mike says, "I'm not sure, but it doesn't go "tick–tock tick–tock" any more. Now it just goes "tick–tick–tick.""

The old man says, "Mmm-Hm!" and steps behind the counter, where he rummages around a bit. He emerges with a

**During their first visit to Dai's local, Janet begins to worry about the future**

huge flashlight and walks over the grandfather clock.

He turns the flashlight on, and shines it directly into the clock's face. Then he says in a menacing voice… "Ve haf vays of making you tock!"

# Marriage

Since the accident, Gareth had been slipping in and out of a coma, yet his wife, Nia stayed by his bedside every single day. When he came to, he motioned for her to come nearer. As she sat by him, he whispered to her, "You've been with me through all the bad times. When I got fired, you were there to support me. When my business went under, you were there. When I got shot, you were there to call the ambulance. When we lost the house to the earthquake, you helped pull me out of the rubble. After the accident, you pulled me from the wreckage before I lost consciousness... Nia, cariad, you're bad luck!"

\*   \*   \*

Ianto and Myfanwy, an elderly couple, meet in a retirement village. They seem to hit it off; they share each other's values, enjoy the same jokes, and find pleasure in each other's company.

After a few months, Ianto asks for the hand of Myfanwy in marriage. She appears hesitant and probes her soon-to-be a little.

"Perhaps I shouldn't look a gift horse in the mouth, but... how's your health?"

"It's OK," Ianto answers. "I'm not getting any younger, but I don't have any major health problems. I can still enjoy life."

"Well, then," Myfanwy replies, "I don't want to be a snoop, but I've got to protect myself: how are you fixed financially?"

"So-so. I'm not rich, but I'm comfortable. You don't have to worry about me sponging off you; I can support myself."

Myfanwy blushed, and finally asks Ianto – "And how's your sex life…"

"Infrequently," he declares.

Myfanwy ponders this for a moment or so, before asking, "And is that one word or two?"

\* \* \*

An efficiency expert concluded his lecture with a note of caution.

"You don't want to try these techniques at home."

"Why not?" asked somebody from the audience.

"I watched my wife's routine at breakfast for years," the expert explained. "She made lots of trips between the refrigerator, stove, table and cabinets, often carrying a single item at a time. One day I told her, 'Love, why don't you try carrying several things at once?'"

"Did it save time?" the person in the audience asked.

"Actually, yes," replied the expert. "It used to take her twenty minutes to make breakfast. Now I do it in seven."

\* \* \*

Ifan was walking down the street when he was accosted by a particularly dirty and shabby-looking tramp, who asked him for a couple of quid for dinner.

Ifan took out his wallet, took out ten pounds and asked, "If I give you this money, will you buy some beer with it instead?"

"No, I had to stop drinking years ago," the tramp replied.

"Will you use it to gamble instead of buying food?" Ifan asked.

"No, I don't gamble," the tramp replied. "I need everything I can get just to stay alive."

"Will you spend this on greens fees at a golf course instead of food?" Ifan asked.

"Are you NUTS!" replied the tramp. "I haven't played golf for twenty years!"

"Will you spend the money on a woman in the red light area instead of food?" Ifan asked.

"What disease would I get for ten quid?!!" exclaimed the tramp.

"Well," said Ifan, "I'm not going to give you the money. Instead, I'm going to take you home for a slap up meal cooked by my wife."

The tramp was amazed. "Won't your wife be furious with you for doing that? I know I'm dirty, and I probably smell pretty disgusting."

Ifan replied, "That's okay. I just want her to see what a man looks like when he's given up beer, gambling, golf, and sex."

\* \* \*

Marriages are made in heaven. But so again, are thunder and lightning.

\* \* \*

If you want your wife to listen and pay strict attention to every word you say, talk in your sleep.

*   *   *

Marriage is grand – and divorce is at least ten grand.

*   *   *

Married life is very frustrating. In the first year of marriage, the man speaks and the woman listens. In the second year, the woman speaks and the man listens. In the third year, they both speak and the neighbours listen.

*   *   *

When a man opens the door of his car for his wife, you can be sure of one thing: either the car is new, or the wife is.

*   *   *

A couple came upon a wishing well. The wife leaned over, made a wish and threw in a penny. The husband decided to make a wish, too. But he leaned over too far, fell into the well, and drowned. The wife was stunned for a moment but then smiled, "It really works!"

*   *   *

Before marriage, a man will lie awake all night thinking about something you say. After marriage, he will fall asleep before you finish.

*   *   *

Every man wants a wife who is beautiful, understanding, economical, and a good cook. But the law allows only one wife.

*   *   *

I recently read that love is entirely a matter of chemistry. That must be why my wife treats me like toxic waste.

*   *   *

A man is incomplete until he is married. After that, he is finished.

*   *   *

Marriage is when a man and woman become as one; the trouble starts when they try to decide which one.

*   *   *

Mrs Ifans decided to have her portrait painted. She told the artist, "Paint me with diamond earrings, a diamond necklace, emerald bracelets and a ruby pendant."

"But, Madam, you are not wearing any of those things."

"Right enough," said Mrs Ifans. "If I should die before my dear Ianto I know he will remarry right away, and I want his new wife to go stark raving mad looking for the jewellery!"

**Is there anyone present who opposes the marriage of Myfanwy Gwladys-Jones and Godfrey Delaware-Smythe…?**

\* \* \*

During a recent public outing, Marged Ann sneaked off to visit a fortune teller of some local repute. In a dark and hazy room, peering into a crystal ball, the mystic delivered grave news.

"There's no easy way to say this, so I'll just be blunt: Prepare yourself to be a widow. Your husband will die a violent and horrible death this year."

Visibly shaken, Marged Ann stared at the woman's lined face, then at the single flickering candle, then down at her hands. She took a few deep breaths to compose herself. She simply had to know. She met the fortune teller's gaze, steadied her voice, and asked her question: "Will I be acquitted?"

\* \* \*

Ianto walks into a post office one day to see a well-dressed middle-aged, balding man standing at the counter methodically placing "Love" stamps on bright pink envelopes with hearts all over them. He then takes out a perfume bottle and starts spraying scent all over them.

His curiosity getting the better of him, Ianto goes up to the balding man and asks him what he is doing. The man says, "I'm sending out 1,000 Valentine cards signed 'Guess who?'"

"But why?" asked Ianto.

"I'm a divorce lawyer," the man replies.

\* \* \*

Twm and his wife were having dinner at a very fine restaurant when an absolutely stunning young woman comes over to their table, gives Twm a big kiss, tells him she'll see him later, and walks away. His wife glares at him and says, "Who was that?!"

"Oh," said Twm, "I can't tell a lie, that was my mistress."

"That's it," said his wife, "I want a divorce."

"Ok," said Twm "but remember, if you get a divorce, there will be no more shopping trips to Paris, no wintering in the Alps, no Jaguar in the garage, and no more Golf club. But the decision is yours."

Just then the wife notices a mutual friend entering the

restaurant with a gorgeous woman. "Who is that woman with Ifan?" she asks.

"That's his mistress," said Twm.

"Ours is much better looking," says the wife.

\*   \*   \*

A Fairy told a married couple: "For being such an exemplary married couple for 25 years, I will give you each a wish."

"I want to travel around the world with my dearest husband," said Myfanwy. The fairy moved her magic stick, and abracadabra! Two tickets appeared in her hands

Now it was the husband's turn.

Ianto thought for a moment and said, "Well, this moment is very romantic, but an opportunity like this only occurs once in a lifetime. So, I'm sorry my love, but my wish is to have a wife 30 years younger than me."

The wife was deeply disappointed but, a wish was a wish. The Fairy made a circle with her magic stick and abracadabra! Suddenly the husband was 90 years old.

\*   \*   \*

One evening, Myfanwy drew her husband's attention to the couple next door and said, "Do you see that couple? How devoted they are? He kisses her every time they meet. Why don't you do that?"

"I would love to," replied Ianto, "but I don't know her well enough."

\*   \*   \*

# Welsh Medical Cases

Dr Jones from Llanon Hospital pulls out a thermometer from his coat pocket, looks at it and says, "Shit, some asshole's pinched my pen!"

*   *   *

Dai goes to a psychiatrist at the Heath. The psychiatrist gives him a Rorschach Test – that is, he shows Dai a circle with a dot inside it and asks, "What do you see?"

Dai replies, "Two people are having sex in the middle of a round room."

The psychiatrist shows Dai another picture, of a square with a dot inside it and asks, "What do you see?"

Dai then answers, "Two people are having sex in a square room."

The psychiatrist shows Dai one more picture, of a triangle with a dot outside it and asks, "What do you see now?"

Dai answers, "Doctor, are you some kind of pervert?!?"

*   *   *

At an international meeting in Bronglais Hospital, two surgeons were having an argument. The Indian surgeon was saying, "No, no, no, I am telling you it is woomba!"

The African surgeon is saying, "No man, it is whoooooom-mmmmm!"

They go on like this for about 10 minutes. Up comes

Ianto, a proud father, from the Maternity wing, and interrupts them. "Excuse me, Sirs, I couldn't help hearing your conversation but I do believe that the word you are trying to say is womb."

After he has gone away, the African turns to the Indian and says, "Who the hell was that know-all? I bet you he has never even seen a hippopotamus, never mind heard one fart under water!

\*　　\*　　\*

While doing a vasectomy, the Dr Thomas slipped and cut off one of Meirion's balls. To avoid a huge malpractice suit, he decides to replace the missing ball with an onion. Several weeks later, Meirion returned for a checkup.

"How's your sex life?" Doctor Thomas asked.

"Pretty good," replied Meirion, to the doctor's relief. Then he added, "But I've had some strange side effects."

"What's that?" Dr Thomas asked him anxiously.

"Well, every time I go to the toilet, my eyes water. When I'm in bed with my wife, she gets heartburn. And every time I pass a hamburger stand, I get an erection!"

\*　　\*　　\*

Dai had been away serving with the army in Bosnia. When he came home he discovered that his wife was eight months pregnant. This worried Dai, as he'd been away for almost eleven months. So he went to have a talk with his doctor.

Dr Jones explained to Dai that this was quite possible, by adding that it was called a grudge pregnancy.

"What sort of pregnancy is that?" enquired Dai.

"Oh," replied the Doctor, "it means that someone had it in for you!"

\* \* \*

Aled was carrying two babies, one in each arm, while waiting for a train. Along came this woman, and upon seeing the two cute babies, she said, "Aren't they cute! What are their names?"

Aled, giving the lady an angry look, replied, "I don't know."

The lady asked again, "Which is a boy and which is a girl?"

Aled, looking angrier than before, replied, "I don't know!"

The woman then started to scold Aled: "What kind of a dad are you?"

Aled answered "Madam, I am not their father, I am just a condom salesman –these are two complaints that I am taking back to my company!"

\* \* \*

Myfanwy goes to her doctor complaining that she is exhausted all the time. After the diagnostic tests showed nothing, the doctor gets around to asking her how often she has intercourse.

"Every Monday, Wednesday, and Saturday," replied Myfanwy.

The doctor advised Myfanwy to cut out Monday.

"I can't," said Myfanwy. "That's the only night I'm home with my husband!"

\* \* \*

Myfanwy goes to a gynaecologist for a check-up. She seems to be very embarrassed and uncomfortable.

"Haven't you been examined like this before?" asks the doctor.

"Many times," giggled Myfanwy, "but never by a doctor!"

\*　\*　\*

Myfanwy boarded a crowded airplane. After putting her luggage into the luggage rack, she started frantically screaming: "Is there a doctor on the plane? Is there a doctor on the plane?"

The other passengers were alarmed, and started looking around to see if a doctor would identify himself.

Finally, a young man began to push his way forward through the crowd to where Myfanwy was standing.

When he reached Myfanwy he quickly said, "Yes, I am a doctor. What can I do for you?"

To which Myfanwy replied: "Would you like to marry my daughter?"

\*　\*　\*

Idwal was rather agitated, stomping around the psychiatrist's office, running his hands through his hair, almost in tears.

"Doctor, my memory's gone. Gone! I can't remember my wife's name. I can't remember my children's names. Can't remember what kind of car I drive. Can't remember where I work. It was all I could do to find my way here!"

"Calm down now, Idwal, you'll make yourself ill! How long have you been like this?"

"Like what?"

*   *   *

Rhian goes to the dentist. In the chair, the dentist notices a little brown spot on one of her teeth.

"Aha, a cavity! I'll have to drill this one out!" says the dentist.

"Oh no!" replies Rhian, " I'd rather have a child!" she cries.

"In that case, I will have to adjust the chair first," replies the dentist.

*   *   *

Marged went to the dentist. As he leans over to begin working on her, she grabs his balls, evoking the comment, "Mrs Thomas, I believe you've got a hold of my privates."

Marged replies, "Yes… And we're going to be careful not to hurt each other, aren't we?"

*   *   *

Ioan complained to his friend Gareth that love-making with his wife was becoming routine and boring.

"Get creative Ioan. Break up the monotony. Why don't you try 'playing doctor' for an hour? That's what I do," said Gareth.

"Sounds great," Ioan replied, "but how do you make it last for an hour?" "That's easy… just keep her in the waiting room for 59 minutes!"

*   *   *

A dietician was once addressing a large audience in Bronglais Hospital.

"The material we put into our stomachs is enough to have killed most of us sitting here years ago. Red meat is awful. Soft drinks erode your stomach lining. Chinese food is loaded with MSG. Vegetables can be disastrous, and none of us realizes the long-term harm caused by the germs in our drinking water. But there is one thing above all that is the most dangerous – and most of us will have eaten it. Can anyone here name the food that causes the most grief and suffering for years after eating it?"

Ianto in the front row stood up and said, "Wedding cake."

*   *   *

Heulwen was having a consultation with her doctor. As they spoke, her little Edwin could clearly be heard terrorizing the people in the waiting room – yet she made no attempt to restrain him.

Soon they heard some clattering in an adjoining room, but still she did nothing. Finally, after an extra-loud crash, the woman casually told the doctor, "I hope you don't mind my little Edwin playing in there."

"No, not at all," said the doctor calmly. "I'm sure he'll calm down as soon as he finds the poison."

Beryl went to the hospital to visit a friend. She had not been in a hospital for several years and felt very ignorant about all the new technology. A technician followed her into the lift, wheeling a large, intimidating-looking machine with tubes and wires and dials.

"Boy, would I hate to be hooked up to that thing," Beryl said.

"So would I," replied the technician. "It's a floor-cleaner."

*   *   *

With the help of a fertility specialist, Megan, a 65-year-old woman, has a baby. All her relatives come to visit and meet the newest member of their family. When they ask to see the baby, Megan says, "Not yet."

A little later, they again ask to see the baby. Again Megan says, "Not yet."

Finally, they say, "When can we see the baby!?" And Megan says, "You'll have to wait until the baby cries."

And they ask, "Why do we have to wait until the baby cries?"

"Because," replies Megan, "I forgot where I put it!"

*   *   *

Ephraim hasn't been feeling well, so he goes to his doctor for a complete checkup.

Afterwards, the doctor comes out with the results.

"I'm afraid, Ephraim, I have some very bad news," the doctor says. "You're dying, and you don't have much time left."

"Oh, that's terrible!" said Ephraim. "How long have I got?"

"Ten," the doctor says sadly. "Ten?" asks Ephraim. "Ten what? Months? Weeks? What?"

"Nine… eight… seven…"

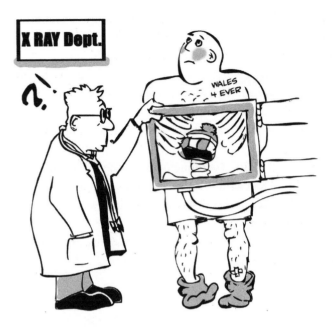

**Alwyn never dreamt that Wales would actually beat the mighty All Blacks...**

\*   \*   \*

"Doc, I can't stop singing 'The Green, Green Grass of Home'."

"That sounds like Tom Jones syndrome."

"Is it common?"

"It's not unusual."

\*   \*   \*

Two elderly couples were enjoying friendly conversation when Ephraim asked the other husband, "Ifan, how was the memory clinic you went to last month?"

"Outstanding," Ifan replied. "They taught us all the latest psychological techniques – visualization, association – it's made a big difference for me."

"That's great! What was the name of that clinic, then, Ifan?"

Ifan went blank. He thought and thought but couldn't remember. Then a smile broke across his face and he asked, "What do you call that flower with the long stem and thorns?"

"You mean a rose?"

"Yes, that's it!" He turned to his wife. "Rose, what was the name of that clinic?"

* * *

Garmon walked into a doctor's surgery and the reception-ist asked, "Can I help you?"

He replied, "I've got shingles."

She said, "Fill out this form and supply your name, address, medical history. When you're done, please take a seat."

Fifteen minutes later, the nurses came out and asked him what he had.

He said, "I've got shingles." So she took down his height, weight, and complete medical history, then said, "Change into this gown and wait in the examining room."

A half hour later another nurse came in and asked him what he had. He said, "I've got shingles." So she gave him a blood test, a blood pressure test, an electrocardiogram, and told him to wait for the doctor.

An hour later the doctor came in and asked Garmon what he had. He said, "Shingles." The doctor gave him a full-cavity examination, and then said, "I just checked you out thoroughly, and I can't find shingles anywhere."

Garmon replied, "They're outside in the back of the lorry. Where do you want them?"

\* \* \*

Ifan had a hell of a car accident and they have to amputate his brain. So the nurse takes him to the brain transplant warehouse.

On one side the shelves are lined with brains marked £200 each.

On the other side the shelves are lined with brains marked £100 each.

Ianto asks why the price differece.

The nurse points to the £100 brains and explains that these are Welsh brains, so they've been used.

\* \* \*

Three elderly ladies were at the doctor for a cognitive reasoning test.

The doctor says to the Mattie, "What is three times three?"

"297," was her prompt reply.

"Ummm humm," says the doc.

The doctor says to the Megan, "It's your turn now. What is three times three?"

"Friday," replied Megan.

"Ummm humm…"

Then the doc says to Myfanwy, the third, "Okay, Myfanwy, your turn. What's three times three?"

"Nine," she says.

"That's wonderful!" says the doc. "Tell me, how did you get that?"

"Simple," she says, beaming. "I subtracted 297 from Friday!"

# Holy

Ifan goes to the confessional and begins "Forgive me, Father, for I have sinned."

"What is your sin, my son?" the priest asks back.

"Well," Ifan goes, "I used some horrible language this week and I feel absolutely terrible."

"When did you use this awful language?" asks the priest.

"I was golfing and hit an incredible drive that looked like it was going to go over 250 yards, but it struck a phone line that was hanging over the fairway and fell straight down to the ground after going only about 100 yards."

"Is that when you swore?"

"No, Father," says Ifan.

"After that, a squirrel ran out of the bushes and grabbed my ball in his mouth and began to run away."

"Is THAT when you swore?" asks the priest again.

"Well, no," replies Ifan.

"You see, as the squirrel was running, a large seagull came down out of the sky, grabbed the squirrel in his claws and began to fly away!"

"Is THAT when you swore?" asks the amazed priest.

"No, not yet," Ifan replies.

"As the seagull carried the squirrel away in his claws, it flew toward the green. As it passed over a a bit of forest near the green, the squirrel dropped my ball."

"Did you swear THEN?" asks the now impatient priest.

"No, because as the ball fell it struck a tree, bounced through some bushes, careened off a big rock, and rolled through a sand trap onto the green and stopped within six inches of the hole."

The priest sighs, "You missed the bloody putt, didn't you?!"

\*   \*   \*

Myfanwy came home and told her Mother that her boyfriend had proposed but she had turned him down because she found out he was an atheist, and didn't believe in Heaven or Hell.

"Marry him anyway, dear," the Mother said. "Between the two of us, we'll show him just how wrong he is."

\*   \*   \*

Did you hear about the three preachers who were talking about their common problem with bats flying in the church?

The first: "I shot at them with a shotgun; but it only spoiled the woodwork."

The second: "I tried a more humane approach, netting them and releasing them 10 miles away. But they beat me back to the church!"

The third (who was looking pretty smug): "I caught them, and baptized and confirmed each one. I haven't seen them since."

\*   \*   \*

Ianto, in an inebriated state, stumbles along to a baptismal service on Sunday afternoon down by the river.

He walked down into the water and stood next to the minister. The minister turns and notices Ianto in a very drunken state and says, "Ianto, are you ready to find Jesus?"

Ianto looked back and says, "Yes, Minister, I sure am."

The minister then dunks Ianto under the water and pulls him right back up. "Have you found Jesus?" the preacher asked.

"Nooo, I haven't!" said Ianto.

The minister then dunks him under for quite a bit longer, brings him up and says, "Now, brother, have you found Jesus?"

"Noooo, I have not, minister."

The minister, in disgust, holds Ianto under for at least 30 seconds this time, brings him out of the water and says in a harsh tone, "My God, man, have you found Jesus yet?"

Ianto wipes his eyes and says to the preacher, "Are you sure this is where he fell in?"

\*     \*     \*

Alun, in his seventies, asked the local priest to hear his confession. "Father, during World War II a beautiful German woman knocked on my door and asked me to hide her from the authorities. I hid her in the attic."

The priest replied, "That was a wonderful thing you did, my son, and you have no need to confess."

"It's worse, Father. I was weak and told her she must repay me with sexual favours," said Alun.

"You were both in great danger," replied the priest. "You would have suffered terribly if the authorities had found her.

Heaven, in its wisdom and mercy, will balance the good and evil, and judge you kindly. You are forgiven."

"Thank you, Father," said the Alun relieved. "That's a great load off my mind. But I have one more question."

"And what is that?" inquired the priest.

"Should I tell her the war is over?" said Alun.

\* \* \*

Bari had a prospective career ahead, and, decided to marry a respectable convent girl, untarnished with the sins of contemporary society. After the wedding service, the bridal couple had to drive through the more unsavoury areas of the city on the way to the reception.

"Bari, what are those women doing leaning against lampposts?"

"Oh, those are just tarts who hire their bodies out for sex at £25 a time."

"Wow, £25!" exclaimed the bride, "the monks only used to give us an apple…"

\* \* \*

Myfanwy took her daughter to the doctor and asked him to give her an examination to determine the cause of her daughter's swollen abdomen. It only took the doctor about two seconds to say "Your daughter is pregnant."

Myfanwy turned red with fury and she argued with the doctor that her daughter was a good girl and would never compromise her reputation by having sex with a boy. The doctor faced the window and silently looked out at the horizon.

Myfanwy became enraged and screamed, "Stop looking out the window! Aren't you paying attention to me?"

"Yes, of course I am paying attention Mrs Jones. It's just that the last time this happened, a star appeared in the East, and three wise men came. If they show up again, I'd like to witness it!"

\*　　\*　　\*

Dai decides to become a monk and ends up in a monastery somewhere off the Pembrokeshire coast. He is assigned to help the other monks in copying the old canons and laws of the church by hand. He notices, however, that all of the monks are copying from copies, not from the original manuscript.

So Dai goes to the chief abbot to question this, pointing out that if someone made even a small error in the first copy, it would never be picked up. In fact, that error would be continued in all of the subsequent copies.

The chief monk, says, "We have been copying from the copies for centuries, but you make a good point, my son."

So, the boss man goes down into the dark caves underneath the monastery where the original manuscript is held with archives in a locked vault that hasn't been opened for hundreds of years.

Hours go by and nobody sees the old abbot. So, Dai gets worried and goes downstairs to look for him.

He sees him banging his head against the wall, and wailing, "We forgot the R, We forgot the R!" His forehead is all bloody and bruised and he is crying uncontrollably.

Dai asks the old man, "What's wrong, father?"

With a choking voice, the old abbot replies, "The word is celebrate. The word is celebRate!"

*   *   *

Priests are so different to other men.
All children call them father, except their own, who call them Uncle!

*   *   *

A monastery in mid-Wales was having a hard time with its cash flow because of the dwindling number of monks available to help with all the work. Then one day, two of the monks, who had been discussing the problem, suggested they open a fish and chips stand down on the highway, right on a scenic route, popular with tourists. The other monks agreed, and the two put up the stand.

One day, a tourist who wanted to offer a compliment, asked the monk on duty, "Are you the fish fryer?"

"No, sir," retorted the brother, "I'm the chip monk."

*   *   *

One day near Llandrindod Wells, three priests went for a hike. It was very hot. They were sweating and were exhausted when they came upon a small lake. Since it was fairly secluded, they took off all their clothes and jumped into the water. Feeling refreshed, the trio decided to pick a few berries while enjoying their 'freedom'. As they were crossing an open area, a group of ladies came along from the town. Unable to get to their clothes in time, two of the priests covered their privates, but the third one covered his face while they ran for cover. After the ladies had left and the men got their clothes back on, the first two priests asked the third why he covered his face rather than his privates. The third replied, "I do not know about you, but in my congregation, it is my face they would recognize."

\* \* \*

A priest from Grangetown is called away for an emergency. Not wanting to leave the confessional unmanned, he calls up a rabbi friend and asks him to cover for him. The rabbi says he wouldn't know what to say, but the priest tells him to come on over and he'll show him what to do. So the rabbi comes over, and he and the priest are in the confessional.

In a few minutes a woman comes in and says, "Father forgive me, for I have sinned."

"What did you do?" the priest asks.

"I committed adultery," the woman says.

"How many times?"

"Three times."

"Say two Hail Marys, put £5 in the box, and go and sin no more."

A few minutes later another woman enters the confessional. She says, "Father forgive me, for I have sinned."

"What did you do?"

"I committed adultery."

"How many times?"

"Three times."

"Say two Hail Marys, put £5 in the box, and go and sin no more."

The rabbi tells the priest that he thinks he's got it, so the priest leaves.

A few minutes later, another woman enters and says, "Father forgive me for I have sinned."

"What did you do?" asks the Rabbi.

"I committed adultery."

"How many times?"

"Just once."

"Go do it two more times," says the Rabbi. "We have a special this week, three for £5."

\* \* \*

A minister walked into a barber shop in Aberaeron. After his haircut, he asked how much it would be. The barber said, "No charge. I consider it a service to the Lord."

The next morning, the barber came to work and there were 12 prayer books and a thank-you note from the minister in front of the door.

Later that day, a policeman came in and got his hair cut. He then asked how much it was. The barber said, "No charge. I consider it a service to the community."

The next morning, he came to work and there were a dozen donuts and a thank-you note from the policeman.

Then, a councillor came in and got a haircut. When he was done he asked how much it was. The barber said, "No charge. I consider it a service to the country."

The next morning, the barber came to work and there were twelve councillors in front of the door.

\* \* \*

A preacher dies, and when he gets to Heaven, he sees a Cardiff taxi driver who has more crowns. He says to an angel, "I don't get it. I devoted my whole life to my congregation." The angel says, "We reward results. Did your congregation always pay attention when you gave a sermon?" The preacher says, "Once in a while someone fell asleep." The angel says, "Right, when people rode in this guy's taxi, they not only stayed awake, but they prayed!"

\*    \*    \*

It seems that when God was making the world, he called man over and bestowed upon him twenty years of normal sex life. Man was horrified: "Only twenty years of normal sex life?" But the Lord was very adamant that was all man could have.

Then the Lord called the monkey and gave him twenty years. "But I don't need twenty years," he protested. "Ten is plenty for me."

Man spoke up eagerly. "Can I have the other ten?" The monkey graciously agreed.

Then the Lord called the lion and gave him twenty years, and the lion, like the monkey, wanted only ten. Again the man spoke up, "Can I have the other ten?" The lion said of course he could.

Then came the donkey and he was given twenty years – but like the others, ten was sufficient – and again man pleaded, "Can I have the other ten?"

This explains why man has twenty years of normal sex life, plus ten years of monkeying around, ten years of lion about it, and ten years of making an ass of himself.

*   *   *

A young Catholic priest on Caldy Island devoted his life to the faith in the monastery. He joined one particularly strict sect. The head monk told him, at his indoctrination, that they were sworn to TOTAL silence. They could not speak one word at all. However, every ten years, they would be permitted to speak two words.

After 10 years of total silence, the head monk indicated it was now time for him to speak his two words. The monk said, "Bed hard!" And then he resumed his silent study and work.

Another 10 years passed and the head monk again indicated it was time for him to speak his two words. The monk said, "Food bad!" And then he resumed his silent study and work.

Another 10 years passed and the head monk again indicated it was time for him to speak his two words. The monk said, "I quit!"

The head monk shook his head and said, "I knew this was coming. You've done nothing but complain for the past 30 years!"

*   *   *

A minister was giving a sermon to a full church when all of a sudden the devil appeared. He was menacing and threatening, and the entire congregation started to flee the church, except for Ianto.

When the church was empty, the devil went up to Ianto and asked, "Aren't you afraid of me? I'm evil incarnate, the

**Even the clergy has to diversify these days**

most horrific being in the universe and will most likely torture you!"

Ianto replied, "You don't scare me. I've been married to your sister for 35 years!"

\* \* \*

One day at a séance meeting in Brynaman, the topic was ghosts. Before the show, the medium asked the congregation "Who here has ever sensed the presence of a ghost?" and five people raised their hand.

Then she asked, "Who here has ever SEEN a ghost?" and three people raised their hands. Then she asked, "Okay, now who here has ever had sex with a ghost?" and one person, an old man, raises his hand.

So she asks the old man, "What was it like?"

"Oh, it was great! Never had any like it before or since!"

"Really? So the ghost was good??"

"Ghost?" says the old man. "I thought you said GOAT!"

\*　　\*　　\*

One Sunday, Ifan walks into a church and kneels down at the altar. He begins to pray to God, saying he owes many people money, and asks to win the lottery. After he is finished, he gets up and walks out.

The next Sunday he goes to the same church and pleads with God through his prayers to let him win the lottery so that he can pay these people back.

The next Sunday comes around, and Ifan enters the church very upset and close to tears. He kneels at the alter and asks why God is doing this to him, saying that he has asked to win the lottery for three weeks – with no result.

Suddenly there is a loud clap of thunder and God speaks: "Ifan, meet me halfway – buy a damn ticket!"

\*　　\*　　\*

One Sunday, a pastor told his congregation that the church in Wales needed some extra money. He asked the people to consider donating a little more than usual, and said that whoever gave the most could choose three hymns.

After the offering plates were passed, the pastor glanced down and noticed that someone had placed a £100 note in one of the plates. He was so excited that he immediately shared his joy with his congregation. He said he'd like to personally thank the person who placed the money in the plate. A very quiet, elderly, saintly-looking lady at the back shyly raised her hand. The pastor asked her to come to the front. Slowly she made her way to the front. The pastor told her how wonderful her gift was, and in thanks, asked her to choose three hymns. Her eyes brightened as she looked over the congregation, pointed to the three most handsome men in the building and said, "I'll take him, and him, and him!"

\* \* \*

A rabbi, a minister, and a priest were playing poker in a Cardiff nightclub when the police raided the game. Turning to the priest, the chief police officer said, "Father Murphy, were you gambling?"

Turning his eyes to heaven, the priest whispered, "Lord, forgive me for what I am about to do." To the police officer, he then said, "No, officer; I was not gambling."

The officer then asked the minister, "Pastor Johnson, were you gambling?"

Again, after an appeal to heaven, the minister replied, "No, officer; I was not gambling."

Turning to the rabbi, the officer again asked, "Rabbi Goldstein, were you gambling?"

Shrugging his shoulders, the rabbi replied, "With whom?"

\* \* \*

Three preachers were discussing the best positions for prayer while Dai was painting the chapel in the same room as them.

"Kneeling is definitely best," claimed one.

"No," another contended. "I get the best results standing with my hands outstretched to Heaven."

"You're both wrong," the third insisted. "The most effective prayer position is lying prostrate, face down on the floor."

Dai, who was painting the chapel, could contain himself no longer. "Hey, fellas," he interrupted, "the best praying I ever did was hanging upside down from a ladder off a three-storey building!"

# Tourists

It was Saturday morning as Emyr, a keen hunter, visiting Aberdeen, woke up ready to go and bag the first deer of the season. He walked down to the kitchen to get a cup of coffee, and to his surprise he found his wife, Sioned, sitting there fully dressed in camouflage.

Emyr asked her, "What are you up to?"

Sioned smiled. "I'm going hunting with you!"

Emyr, though he had many reservations about this, reluctantly decided to take her along. Later they arrived at the hunting site. Emyr set Sioned safely up in the tree stand and told her, "If you see a deer, take careful aim and I'll come running back as soon as I hear the shot."

Emyr walked away with a smile on his face, knowing that Sioned had no chance in hell of seeing a deer, let alone shooting one. A quarter of an hour had passed, when he was startled as he heard a volley of gunshots.

Quickly, Emyr ran back. As he got closer to her stand, he heard Sioned screaming: "Get away from my deer!"

Confused, Emyr raced faster towards his screaming wife. And again he heard her yell: "Get away from my deer!" followed by another volley of gunfire!

Now within sight of where he had left his wife, Emyr was surprised to see a Scotsman in jodhpurs with his hands high in the air. The Scotsman, obviously distraught, said, "Och aye, lady, och aye! You can have your deer! Just let me get my saddle off it!"

*    *    *

A big earthquake with a strength of 8.1 on the Richter scale has hit England.

Two million English have died and over a million are injured. The country is totally ruined and the government doesn't know where to start with providing help to rebuild. The rest of the world is in shock.

Canada is sending troopers to help the English army control the riots.

Saudi Arabia is sending oil.

Latin American countries are sending supplies.

The European community (except France) is sending food and money.

Wales, not to be outdone, is sending two million replacement Englishmen.

Cymru am Byth!

*    *    *

D ai was flying to Alicante when, after the aeroplane reached a comfortable cruising altitude, the captain made an announcement over the intercom, "Ladies and gentlemen, this is your captain speaking. Welcome to Flight 293, non-stop from Cardiff to Alicante. The weather ahead is good and therefore we should have a smooth and uneventful flight. Now, please sit back and relax – OH MY GOD!"

Silence. Then, the captain came back on the intercom and said, "Ladies and Gentlemen, I'm so sorry if I scared you, but while I was talking, the flight-attendant brought me a cup of coffee and spilled the hot coffee in my lap. You should see the front of my pants!"

Dai piped up, "That's nothing… You should see the back of mine!"

* * *

On doctor's orders, Idwal had moved to Spain. Two weeks later, he was dead. His body was shipped back home, where the undertaker prepared it for the service. Idwal's brother Ithel came in to make sure everything was taken care of.

"Would you like to see the body?" the undertaker asked.

"I might as well, before the others get here." The undertaker led him into the next room and opened the top half of the casket. He stood back and proudly displayed his work.

"He looks good," Ithel said. "Those two weeks in Spain were just the thing for him."

* * *

Ianto finally decided to take a holiday. He was tired of all the cold and snow on his farm in mid-Wales, so he booked himself on a Caribbean cruise and proceeded to have the time of his life – until the boat sank.

He found himself swept up on the shore of an island with no other people, no supplies… nothing, only bananas and coconuts. After about four months, he was lying on the beach one day when the most gorgeous woman he had ever seen rowed up to him. In disbelief, Ianto asked her, "Who are you? Where did you come from? How did you get here?"

She replied, "I'm Myfanwy and I rowed over from the

other side of the island," she said. "I landed here when my cruise ship sank."

"Amazing," he said. "You were really lucky to have a rowing boat wash up with you."

"Oh, this?" replied Myfanwy. "I made the rowing boat out of raw material found on the island. I whittled the oars from gum tree branches, I wove the bottom from palm branches, and the sides and stern came from a Eucalyptus tree."

"But that's impossible!" stuttered Ianto. "You had no tools or hardware! How did you manage?"

"Oh, that was no problem," replied Myfanwy. "On the south side of the island, there is a very unusual strata of alluvial rock exposed. I found if I fired it to a certain temperature in my kiln, it melted into forgeable ductile iron. I used that for tools and used the tools to make the hardware."

Ianto was amazed. "Let's row over to my place," she said.

After a few minutes of rowing, she docked the boat at a small wharf. As Ianto looked onto shore, he nearly fell out of the boat. Before him was a stone walk leading to an exquisite bungalow painted in red and green. While the woman tied up the rowboat with an expertly woven hemp rope, he could only stare ahead, dumbstruck. As they walked into the house, she said casually, "It's not much, but I call it home. Sit down please; would you like to have a drink?"

"No, thank you," he said, still dazed. "I can't face any more coconut juice."

"It's not coconut juice," the woman replied. "I built a distillery. How do you fancy a Pina Colada?"

Trying to hide his continued amazement, Ianto accepted, and they sat down on her hand-woven couch to talk. After they had exchanged their stories, Myfanwy announced, "I'm

**Misunderstood locals chat away
in their native Welsh tongue**

going to slip into something more comfortable. Would you like to take a shower and shave? There is a razor upstairs in the cabinet in the bathroom."

Without hesitation, Ianto went into the bathroom. There, in the cabinet, was a razor made from a bone handle. Two shells honed to a hollow ground edge were attached to its end, inside a swivel mechanism.

"WOW! Myfanwy is truly amazing," he mused, "what next?"

When he returned, Myfanwy was there to greet him wearing nothing but vines strategically positioned, and smelling faintly of lilac. She beckoned for him to sit down next to her.

"Tell me," she began suggestively, slithering closer to him, "We've been out here for a really long time. I know you've been really lonely, Ianto, but so have I, you know, and I'm sure there's something you really feel like doing right now, something you've been longing for all these months. You know…" She stared lovingly, longingly, into his eyes.

Ianto couldn't believe what he was hearing. "You mean…" he swallowed excitedly, "you've got a dart board here?!"

\* \* \*

Dai got a job on an ocean liner as a conjuror and magician, and, on performing one night, the Captain's parrot kept on interrupting his act by giving his secrets of the trade away with comments such as "It's up his sleeve, it's behind his ear," and so on.

Whatever trick Dai performed, the parrot kept his beady eye on it and gave the show away to the audience.

One evening, during the show, the ship hit an iceberg and started to sink.

Dai managed to jump overboard and find a plank to cling onto. Soon afterwards, the parrot lands on the same plank.

For the next two days, they just stared at one another, until in the end the parrot chirps, "OK, I give up, what have you done with the ship?"

\* \* \*

Dai gets on a plane and sits next to the window. A few minutes later, a big, heavy, strong, mean-looking guy sits down in the seat next to him and immediately falls asleep.

Dai starts to feel a little airsick, but he's afraid to wake the big guy up to ask if he can move aside to let him go to the loo. He knows he can't climb over him, and so Dai is sitting there, looking at the big guy, trying to decide what to do.

Suddenly, the plane hits an air pocket and an uncontrollable wave of nausea passes through Dai. He can't hold it in any longer and hurls all over the big guy's chest.

About five minutes later the big guy wakes up, looks down, and sees the vomit all over him.

"So," says Dai, "are you feeling any better now?"

*   *   *

Ianto was walking along Penarth beach when he found a bottle. When he rubbed it, lo and behold, a genie appeared.

"I will grant you three wishes," announced the genie. "But since Satan still hates me, for every wish you make, your rival, Brynley, gets the wish as well – only double!"

Ianto thought about this for a while. "For my first wish, I would like ten million quid," he announced.

Instantly the genie gave him a Swiss bank account number and assured him that 10 million had been deposited. "But Brynley has just received 20 million," the genie said.

"I've always wanted a Ferrari," Ianto said.

Instantly a Ferrari appeared. "But Brynley has just received two Ferraris," the genie said. "And what is your last wish?"

"Well," said Ianto, "I've always wanted to donate a kidney for transplant."

*   *   *

# Naughty Section

Gareth, a Llanbrynmair farmer had been screwing one of his sheep for five years, when all of a sudden he was hit by pangs of conscience.

It bothered him so much that in the end he decided that he just had to tell his wife about it.

Now Nia was so shocked and could only say to Gareth, "Well, was the pig a male or a female?"

"A female, of course!" shouted Gareth. "What do you think I am – some sort of queer?"

*   *   *

And then there's little Emyr, who woke up one night to go the bathroom, and passed by his parents' door.

Noticing that the door was open a bit, he walked in, only to see his mother performing oral sex on his dad.

Upon seeing this, little Johnny walks out and exclaims –

"Huh! They've got a nerve! They sent me to the doctor for sucking my thumb!"

*   *   *

One day a mother and father were having sex, and their son Tomi walked in. "What are you doing?" he asked. "Well, you wanted a brother, so we're making you one." The next day, the father walks outside and sees little Tomi porking away on the family car's exhaust pipe.

"Tomi… what the bloody hell are you doing!!!"

And Tomi replied, "Mammy said she wanted a new car, so I'm making her one!"

*   *   *

A group of people were in a shipwreck and were stranded on an island.

The group consisted of twelve women and Ianto. After a few months, the women grew horny and it was decided that Ianto should take two women a day, with Sundays off.

One day on a day off, he was just relaxing when he noticed a boat nearing. He felt hopeful that maybe they would be rescued, at last.

The boat was almost to the island when the Ianto noticed it was a man in the boat. As he got out, Ianto said, "Oh my God butty, am I ever glad to see you!"

To which the man responded, "Well alright, sweetie! It's been a long time for me too!"

Ianto sighed, "Oh hell, there go my Sundays!"

*   *   *

A solicitor married the well-to-do Betsan, who had previously divorced nine husbands, so he became her tenth. On their wedding night, Betsan implored her new husband, "Please be gentle; I'm still a virgin."

"What?" said the puzzled groom. "How come, if you've been married so many times before?

"Well," she replied, "Husband Number 1 was a Sales

Representative; he kept telling me how great it was going to be.

Husband Number 2 was in Software Services; he was never really sure how it was supposed to function, but he said he'd look into it and get back to me, but he just couldn't get the system up.

Husband No 3 was in Telemarketing; even though he knew he had the order, didn't know when he would be able to deliver.

Husband No 4 was an Engineer; he understood the basic process but wanted three years to research, implement, and design a new state-of-the-art method.

Husband No 5 was from Finance and Administration; he thought he knew how, but he wasn't sure whether it was his job or not.

Husband No 6 was in Marketing; although he had a product, he was never sure how to position it.

Husband No 7 was a psychiatrist; all he ever did was talk about it.

Husband No 8 was a gynaecologist; all he did was look at it.

Husband No 9 was a stamp collector; all he ever did was… God, I miss him!

But now that I've married you, I'm really excited!"

"Good," said the husband, "but, why?"

"You're a Solicitor. This time I KNOW I'm going to get screwed!"

*   *   *

One day, the farmer's widow said to the stockman, Wil, "You've done a really good job and the farm looks really good. You should go into town and kick up your heels." Wil readily agreed and went into Aberystwyth one Saturday night.

However, one o'clock came and he didn't return. Two o'clock, and no Wil. He returned around two-thirty and found the farmer's widow sitting by the fireplace. She quietly called him over to her.

"Unbutton my blouse and take it off," she said. Trembling, Wil did as he was told.

"Now take off my boots." Wil did so, slowly.

"Now take off my socks." He did.

"Now take off my skirt." He did.

"Now take off my bra." Again, with trembling hands, Wil did as he was told.

"Now," she said, "take off my panties." He slowly pulled them down and off.

Then she looked at him and said, "Wil, if you ever wear my clothes to Aberystwyth again, I'll sack you on the spot."

\*   \*   \*

While I was flying down the road yesterday (only 15 mph over), I noticed a policeman with a radar gun sitting on top of a bridge.

Naturally, he pulled me over, walked up to the car and asked me, "What's the hurry?"

I replied, "I'm late for work."

"Oh yeah," said the officer. "What do you do?"

"I'm a rectum stretcher," I responded.

The officer said, "What? A rectum stretcher? What does a rectum stretcher do?"

I said, "Well, I start with one finger, then I work my way up to two fingers, then three, then four, then my whole hand. Then I work until I can get both hands in there, and then I slowly stretch it until it's about 6 foot wide."

The officer asked me, "What the hell do you do with a 6 foot asshole?"

I simply replied, "You give him a radar gun and park him on top of a bridge."

*　　*　　*

Gareth, in his 85th year, went to his doctor's surgery to get a sperm count. The doctor gave Gareth a jar and said, "Take this jar home and bring back a semen sample tomorrow."

The next day Gareth reappeared at the doctor's surgery and gave him the jar, which was as clean and empty as on the previous day. The doctor asked what happened and Gareth explained: "Well, doctor, it's like this – first I tried with my right hand, but nothing. Then I tried with my left hand, but still nothing. Then I asked my wife Megan for help. She tried with her right hand, then her left, still nothing. She tried with her mouth, first with the teeth in, then with her teeth out, and still nothing.

We even called up Eirlys, the woman next door and she tried too, first with both hands, then an armpit and she even tried squeezing it between her knees, but still nothing."

The doctor was shocked. "You asked your neighbour, Eirlys?"

Gareth replied, "Yes. And no matter what we tried, we still couldn't get the bloody jar open!"

**Sam was feeling a bit left out…**

\*    \*    \*

Myfanwy walks into a chemist shop in Pontardulais and asks the shop assistant if he sells size extra large condoms. She replied, "Yes, we do. Would you like to buy some?" Myfanwy replies, "No, madam, but do you mind if I wait around here until someone does?"

\*    \*    \*

A young female teacher was giving her class of six year olds a quiz. "Behind my back I've got something red and round, and you can eat it. What is it?" she asked.

"An apple" replied little Raymond.

"No," said the teacher, "it's a tomato, but it shows you're thinking." "I've now got something round and greenish-colored, and you can eat it."

"An apple," replied little Ian.

"No, it's an onion, but it shows you're thinking."

Little scruffy Tomi at the back of the class says, "I've got something under my desk that's an inch long, white and it has a red end."

"Dirty little boy!" said the teacher.

"No, it's a match – but it shows you're thinking!" he answered.

\* \* \*

Evan wakes up one morning to find a gorilla on his roof. So he looks in the yellow pages and sure enough, there's an ad for Gorilla Removers. He calls the number, and the gorilla remover says he'll be over in 30 minutes. The gorilla remover arrives, and gets out of his van. He's got a ladder, a baseball bat, a shotgun and a mean old pit bull.

"What are you going to do?" Evan asks.

"I'm going to put this ladder up against the roof, then I'm going to go up there and knock the gorilla off the roof with this baseball bat. When the gorilla falls off, the pit bull is trained to grab his balls and not let go. The gorilla will then be subdued enough for me to put him in the cage in the back of the van." He hands the shotgun to the homeowner.

"What's the shotgun for?" asks the concerned and confused Evan.

"If the gorilla knocks me off the roof, shoot the pit bull."

\* \* \*

# Welsh
# Valleys
# Humour

## David
## Jandrell

A first-time visitor to the south Wales Valleys will be subjected to a language that will initially be unfamiliar to them. This book features a tongue-in-cheek guide to the curious ways in which Valleys inhabitants use English, together with anecdotes, jokes, stories depicting Valleys life, and malapropisms from real-life Valleys situations!

*"What a delight David Jandrell's book is!"*
– **Ronnie Barker**

**£3.95**

ISBN: 0 86243 736 9

The *It's Wales* series is just one of
a whole range of Welsh interest
publications from Y Lolfa. For a full list
of books currently in print, send now for
your free copy of our new, full-colour
Catalogue – or simply surf into our
website, **www.ylolfa.com**, for secure,
on-line ordering.

Talybont, Ceredigion, Cymru SY24 5HE
*e-bost* ylolfa@ylolfa.com
*gwefan* www.ylolfa.com
*ffôn* (01970) 832 304
*ffacs* 832 782